Morocco

Your Ultimate Guide to Travel, Culture, History, Food and More!

By Jean Young

Experience Everything Travel Guide Collection™

EXPERIENCE EVERYTHING PUBLISHING

Forward

Thank you for purchasing this book from the Experience Everything Travel Guide Collection™! Inside you will find a ton of useful and entertaining information on Morocco and it is our desire that this book will provide you with the inspiration to explore!

Disclaimer

While this book contains a great deal of information, it does not have all of the information that is available on the Internet. It is written to inspire you about the destination rather than act as a full travel guide that you could use to get from point A to point B or to specific addresses/locations during your tour.

This document is geared towards providing exact and reliable information in regards to the topic and issue covered. The publication is sold with the idea that the publisher is not required to render accounting, officially permitted, or otherwise, qualified services. If advice is necessary, legal or professional, a practiced individual in the profession should be ordered.

- From a Declaration of Principles which was accepted and approved equally by a Committee of the American Bar Association and a Committee of Publishers and Associations:

Introduction

Chapter 1: Geography

    Where is Morocco located? What countries/lands border it?

    How diverse is the ecosystem of Morocco? How is its biodiversity?

    What is the total population?

    What is the weather like?

Chapter 2: The Fascinating History of Morocco

    Etymology Of The Name Morocco

    The Different Dynasties That Ruled Morocco

    Independence of Morocco

    The Kings That Ruled Morocco

    Morocco Politics Today

Chapter 3: The Unique Culture of Morocco

    Languages Spoken

    Different Ethnic Groups

    General Way Of Life: Family Values, and Etiquette and Customs

    Moroccan Religion

    Forms of Entertainment – Music, Sports, Architecture And Literature

Chapter 4: Modes of Transportation in Morocco

Grand Taxis/Petit Taxis

Trains

Buses

Ferries

Bicycles

Chapter 5: Some Cities Of Morocco That You Can Stay At During Your Visit

Rabat

Casablanca

Marrakesh

Chapter 6: Delicious Cuisine And Places To Go To In Those Capitals

Rabat

Casablanca

Marrakesh

Chapter 7: Major Events And Festivals You Should Not Miss!

Marathon des Sables

Rose Festival

Fes Festival

Essaouira Gnawa and World Music Festival

Marrakech Popular Arts Festival

Eid ul-Adha

Introduction

Do you want to go on a unique vacation and visit some beautiful places? Do you want to take a break from your everyday life, and go someplace where you can experience a brand new culture, meet new people, savor delicious food and see beautiful sights? Well, there are definitely countless of countries that you can choose from, but one country that you should certainly consider is Morocco.

Morocco is a very beautiful country that is known for its rich history, beautiful expanse of deserts, regal imperial cities, wonderful beaches and breathtaking riads (riads are traditional palaces or houses that have gardens in its interior). However, Morocco is also known for its unique culture, polite people, delicious cuisines, and amazing festivals!

Although Morocco has had its fair share of difficulties in the past – struggling to gain its independence from the dynasties that dominated it, at present, it has flourished into a beautiful country. So if ever you are looking for a unique destination, you should certainly consider the beautiful Kingdom of Morocco! In order to learn more about its rich history, geography, culture, politics, proprieties and customs, festivals and etc., make sure to cautiously read and scrutinize this guide!

Chapter 1: Geography

If you are interested in visiting Morocco, then you should be familiar where it is, geographically speaking. Not only that, but you should also know what countries or lands border it so that if ever you decide to tour around, then you would not be so lost. In order to learn more about the geography and some other important statistical data of Morocco, just keep on reading!

Where is Morocco situated? What countries/lands border it?

Officially known as the Kingdom of Morocco, this beautiful country is located at North Africa in the Maghreb region. Geographically, it is known by its rugged and mountainous interior, and a wide expanse of desert. Also, did you know that among all the countries in the world, Morocco (along with France and Spain), are the only three to have both Mediterranean and Atlantic coastlines? In fact, Morocco has a coast near the Atlantic Ocean that can reach beyond the Strait of Gibraltar straight into the Mediterranean Sea. It is also bordered by Spain in the north. This is a water border that goes through the land borders and the Strait with three different exclaves that are Spanish-controlled.

These exclaves are Peñón de Vélez de la Gomera, Melila and Ceuta. To the south of Morocco, it is bordered by the Western Sahara and to the east, it is bordered by Algeria. Additionally since Morocco controls majority of the Western Sahara, its southern boundary is then Mauritania in effect.

Internationally, the acknowledged borders of Morocco lie between longitudes 1° and 14°W and latitudes 27°and 36°N. Also when you add Western Sahara, the borders of Morocco then lie mostly between 1° and 17°W and 21° and 36°N. With these official borders, Morocco has a total area of roughly 446,550 km², or 172,410 square miles. Also, although the largest city in Morocco is Casablanca, the city of

Rabat is considered as the political capital of Morocco. Some other major cities include Tetouan, Marrakesh, Oujda, Nador, Kenitra, Fes, Tangier, Agadir, and Meknes.

The topography in Morocco also varies since its interior regions and northern coast are mountainous. Additionally, its coast features includes fertile plains where majority of their agriculture takes place. There are also several valleys scattered between the mountainous areas of Morocco. Jebel Toubkal, the highest point in Morocco stands tall at 4, 165 meters (13,665 feet)! Alternatively, Sebkha Tah its lowest point, only stands below sea level at about -55 meters (-180 feet).

How diverse is the ecosystem of Morocco? How is its biodiversity?

The biodiversity of Morocco is comprised of over 7,000 vegetal species and over 24,000 animal species. Also, the rate of endemism is predominantly high in Mediterranean countries with over 11% for fauna and 20% for vascular plants. The marine and forest ecosystems of Morocco are also particularly rich. In fact, did you know that Morocco is among the highest ranking countries because of its high levels of diversity of fish?

Also, the desert ecosystems of Morocco present around 750 different kinds of vegetal species, 60 of which are considered endemic. It also presents 650 kinds of invertebrates, and around 250 different kinds of birds. Lastly, the Moroccan agricultural ecosystems are widely spread at roughly 8.7 million ha which hosts a wide variety of local races that are supported by traditional practices and knowledge.

However, the trend for the natural assets in Morocco is going downhill. Meaning, it is slowly getting lost and becoming degraded. Presently, there are already around 600 identified endangered species throughout the country! In fact, the degradation rate for some of these species is already irreversible no matter what they do. This is especially true for endangered species found in the Central region for Rif and located around the different capital cities.

Similarly, according to a national study, of the 7,000 taxa that comprise the fauna of Morocco around 1,700 of them are already considered rare and some are even threatened already. If this trend goes on, roughly around 24% of the plant diversity of Morocco will be lost! However, Moroccan authorities, scientists, researchers and even citizens are doing their best to counter this potential loss.

What is the total population?

As of the year 2015, Morocco has a total current population of 33, 696, 722. Out of this total population, 49% are male, that is roughly around 16, 509, 340, while 51% are female that is roughly around 17, 187, 382. The current total population of Morocco has actually increased by 1.07%, that is 354, 445 people compared to the population last 2014 where there were only 33, 218, 847. Also, this increase is a positive since the number of births surpassed the number of deaths by around 479, 680.

The population density at Morocco is at around 75.2 people for every square kilometer. The density of a population is calculated by dividing the number of people who are permanently settled at Morocco from the whole area of the country. Also, the total (whole) area of the country is the sum of the water and land areas that is found within the international coastlines and boundaries of Morocco.

What is the weather like?

For majority of the year in Morocco, it is typically sunny and hot. In fact, during the peak of the summer months it gets unpleasantly hot particularly in Fes, Marrakech and in the southwest part of Morocco all towards the desert. Essaouira, Cablanca and Rabat experience a more comfortable time during the peak of the summer season since they experience the cool ocean breeze.

During November to February, Morocco also experiences winter. And although the winter season that they experience is only mild, the temperatures at night can drop up to 10Celsius (40Fahrenheit)! Also, finding a coating of snow in Northern Morocco is not unusual. In fact, the Atlas Mountains get plenty of snow! If you want, you can even go skiing in Oukaimeden which is located right outside of Marrakech.

Chapter 2: The Fascinating History Of Morocco

Now that you know the physical aspects such as the geographical location and ecosystem of Morocco, and now that you have an idea about its population and weather, you should also know its history. Why should you? Well, knowing the history of Morocco will definitely help you appreciate it for what it is now. Keep on reading and find out some interesting historical facts about Morocco!

Etymology Of The Name Morocco

Morocco is not just known as the Kingdom of Morocco. In fact, it is also known by its full Arabic name *al-Mamlakah al-Maghribiyyah* (المملكة المغربية) which translates to "Kingdom of the West". However for historical purposes, some medieval geographers and historians called Morocco as *al-Maghrib al-Aqṣá* (الأقصى المغرب) which means "The Farthest West". They did this to differentiate it from other neighboring regions called *al-Maghrib al-Adná* (الأدنى المغرب) which means "The Nearest West" and *al-Maghrib al-Awsaṭ* (الأوسط المغرب) which means "The Middle West".

The English name of Morocco originated from the Portuguese and Spanish names "Marrocos" and "Marruecos" respectively. In turn, these names were also a derivative from the Medieval Latin name "Marrakesh" which was once the former Almohad Caliphate capital and Almoravid dynasty from ancient Morocco. Alternatively in Persian, the name Marrakesh remains the same name for Morocco, but that changed in Middle Eastern Arabic later on in the 20th century.

The Different Dynasties That Ruled Morocco

The kingdom of Morocco is a beautiful country that has a very rich and interesting history. There have been various rulers and dynasties that have ruled the country and in turn, influenced the cultural diversity of Morocco. However, the very first inhabitants of Morocco were the Berber people. In order to learn more about the history of Morocco and the different dynasties that ruled it, let us take a trip down memory lane.

First of all, the earliest Moroccan state to be independent was the Berber Kingdom of Mauretania which was ruled by King Bocchus I. This kingdom which was located in the north part of Morocco, dates back to 110 BC, therefore it should not be confused with the present state Mauritania. Also, take note that although there were different dynasties that came and went, the Berber people were the very first inhabitants of Morocco.

Roman Empire

The Empire of Rome controlled the Moroccan region from 1st Century BC and they originally named it Mauretania Tingitana. During the 2nd Century AD, they introduced Christianity and were able to convert towns of people. However, during the 5th Century AD, the Roman Empire started to decline and it was then that the region was invaded by Vandals then next, by the Visigoths. During 6th Century AD, the north part of Morocco became nominally a part of the Byzantine Empire.

Era of Early Islams

During 670 AD, the very first Islamic invasion of the coastal plain of North Africa was led by Uqba ibn Nafi. He was a general who served under the Umayyads of Damascus. These Umayyad Muslims took their government system, their language, and their Islamic ways to Morocco. In fact, many Berber people started to slowly convert to Islam, majority of which happened once the rule of the Arabas regressed.

The very first Muslim independent state in the modern Morocco area is the Kingdom of Nekor – this is an emirate located in the Rif Mountains. It was originally established by Salih I ibn Mansur back in 710 as a state client to Rashidun Caliphate. However, after the Great Berber Revolt back in 739, many Berber people started to form their own independent states like the Barghawata and Miknasa of Sijilmasa.

In fact Idris ibn Abdallah, according the some medieval legend, fled to Morocco once his tribe in Iraq was massacred by the Abbasids. According to the legends, he convinced the Berber Awraba tribes to cut their loyalty to the distant caliphs of Abbasid in Baghdad. Instead, he instituted the Idrisid Dynasty back in 788.

Dynasties Of The Berbers

During the 11 Century and onwards, a succession of powerful Berber dynasties came into power. In fact, under the dynasty of Almoravid, and under the dynasty of Almohad, Morocco was able to dominate Maghreb. They were also able to conquer majority of present-day Portugal and Spain and also the west portion of the Mediterranean region.

During the 13th Century and 14th Century, the Merinids also held some power in Morocco and they endeavored to copy the success of the Almohads in the past by using military campaigns in Spain and Algeria. After the Merinids, they were followed by the Wattasids. During the 15th Century, the Muslim rule that reigned in the southern and central parts of Spain and Portugal came to a stop with the help of the Rencoquista. When this happened, many Jews and Muslims eventually fled to Morocco for home.

Dynasties Of The Sharifian

Back in 1549, Morocco fell to consecutive Arab dynasties. These dynasties claimed that they were descenders of Muhammad, the Islamic prophet. The first Arab Dynasty was the Saadi Dynasty and they ruled Morocco from 1549 to 1659. After them came the Alaouite Dynasty who ruled for a somewhat long time. In fact, they were able to remain in control since the 17th Century.

Under the rule of the Saadi Dynasty, Morocco resisted incursions by Ottomans. However, a Portuguese invasion and a battle of Ksar el Kebir occurred in 1578. Instead, the control of Ahmad al-Mansur brought new prestige and wealth to the Sultanate and a big expedition to the West part of Africa brought the Songhay Empire down in 1591. After this defeat, managing the Sahara territories became too hard and after the demise of al-Mansur, the country was then divided among his sons.

Dynasty of Alaouite

The divided country of Morocco was once again reunited under the Alaouite Dynasty back in 1666. Ever since then, this dynasty became the ruling house in Morocco. At this time, Morocco was facing aggressive attacks from the Ottoman Empire and from Spain. However, the Alaouites were able to stabilize their position and although the kingdom was still smaller compared to the preceding ones in the region, it still remained fairly wealthy.

Back in 1777, Morocco was the first country to recognize the young United States as an independent nation. However, during the start of the American Revolution, merchant ships from America were attacked by Barbary pirates as they passed the Atlantic Ocean. But on December 20, 1777m Sultan Mohammed III of Morocco stated that merchant ships owned by Americans would be placed under his protection. He stated that these American ships cannot be attacked and that they should be able to pass safely and unharmed. Because of this, the Moroccan-American Friendship Treaty was signed back in 1786 and it remains as one of the oldest non-broken treaty of friendship signed by the United States.

Independence of Morocco

Morocco was also invaded by the French however in March 1956, the French colony and rule was ended. This was possible once France allowed Mohammed V to return to Morocco 1955. With his return, negotiations occurred and the Moroccan people gained their independence the following year. During 1956, Morocco gained its freedom from France and re-established itself as the "Kingdom of Morocco". Furthermore, about a month later on, Spain also relinquished majority of its protectorate in the northern parts of Morocco to the brand new state. However, Spain decided to keep two of its coastal enclaves, Melilla and Ceuta, which is located on the Mediterranean coastline.

The Kings That Ruled Morocco

Just as there were different dynasties to conquer Morocco, there were also different Kings who led those empires. Here is a short list of the notable kings to rule Morocco.

Sultan Mohammed. Upon his return, he negotiated with the French and helped Morocco in gaining its freedom. Eventually in 1957, once Morocco was free from its previous colonizers, Sultan Mohammed became the king.

Hassan II. After the death of King Mohammed, Hassan II assumed the throne and became the King of Morocco back in March 9, 1961. Also, Morocco held its very first elections in 1963 but Hassan announced a state of emergency and he suspended the parliament in 1965. Later on in 1971, there was an unsuccessful attempt at deposing King Hassan II in order to establish Morocco as a republic country. Under his reign, a truth commission was set up in 2005 in order to investigate abuses of human rights. During the investigation, 10,000 confirmed cases were found and these cases ranged from forced exile to death while in custody. Also as discovered by the truth commission, during the rule of Hassan, around 592 people were killed. Further disputes occurred however in 1998, the first government-led opposition came to power.

King Mohammed VI. He is the son of King Hassan II and when his father died in 1999. He immediately assumed the throne. He is known as a vigilant modernizer and he introduced social and economic liberalization in his rule.

Morocco Politics Today

Moroccan Government

Ruled by King Mohammed VI since he ascended to power in 1999, Morocco is considered as an autocratic monarchy. It is a constitutional monarchy and it is overseen under the amended 1972 constitution.

Basically, the king holds all effective power and he alone gets to appoint the prime minister. However, there is also the bicameral parliament which is consisted of 270 different seated Chamber of Counselors. The members of this chamber are chosen through indirect voting and their term lasts for nine years. Then, there is also the 325 different seated Chamber of Representatives. The members of chamber are chosen through popular votes and their term lasts for five years. Administratively speaking, the country is divided into fifteen different regions.

The king, King Mohammed VI, alone has the power to appoint all military heads, prime ministers, and the king also serves as the spiritual leader of the nation. Also, majority of political parties that are religion-based are banned in order to prevent any Islamic parties from acquiring any influence. Basically, the 395-seat of Morocco national assembly is essentially powerless against the king.

Moroccan Government At A Quick Glance

Government Type: Constitutional Monarchy

Head of the State: King Mohammed VI

Head of the Government: Prime Minister Abbas EL FASSI (appointed by the king since September 19, 2007)

Constitution: Bicameral Legislature (according to the amended March 1972 constitution, revised in September 1992 and in September 1996)

Year independence was gained: March 2, 1956

Branches: Executive (King as the head of state), Prime Minister (as the head of the government)

Legislative: Judicial (Supreme Court), Bicameral Parliament

Chapter 3: The Unique Culture Of Morocco

Now that you know all about the geography and history of Morocco, it is time for you to learn about its unique culture! To learn more about the language they speak, their general way of life, their etiquettes and societal norms, and religion, keep on reading!

Languages Spoken

The official languages spoken at Morocco are Berber and Arabic. However, there is a distinctive group of Moroccan Arabic dialects and it is referred as Darija. Roughly around 89.8% of the entire Moroccan population can speak and communicate in some degree using Moroccan Arabic.

The Berber language can be spoken in three different dialects namely Central Atlas Tamzight, Tarifit, and Tashelhit. In fact in 2008, Frédéric Deroche assessed that there are around 12 million speakers of Berber that is around 40% of the entire Moroccan population!

Another commonly used language is French. In fact in the media, in government institutions, and even in mid- to large companies, the French language is widely used. This is to allow them to conduct international commerce with other countries that mainly speak French and to allow for international diplomacy. Due its many uses, French is in fact a mandatory language subject taught at all Moroccan schools! A census conducted in 2010 showed that there were about 10,400,000 Moroccans who are also French-speakers – that is around 33% of their entire population!

However, according to another census which was conducted back in 2004, around 2.19 million Moroccans could speak another foreign language aside from French. Second to French, a few number of Moroccan citizens can also speak English. A small population of Moroccans also speaks Spanish. This is especially true in the northern part of Morocco around the Spanish enclaves Ceuta and Melilla.

Different Ethnic Groups

Majority of Moroccans are mostly mixed Arab-Berbers. However, some studies show that there are no radical differences in genetics between non-Arabic and Arabic speaking populations. In fact, an HLA DNA analysis also suggest that majority of Moroccans are of Berber origin. They also suggest that the Arabs who invaded Spain and North Africa during the 7th Century did not significantly add to the gene pool. However, polls conducted last 2014 shows that around 99% of Moroccans are Arab-Berber in ethnicity and only 1% is some other ethnic group.

General Way Of Life: Family Values, and Etiquette and Customs

The general way of life of Moroccans revolves around their most valued possession – their dignity and honor. In accordance to this, Moroccans will definitely do their very best to preserve whatever personal honor that they hold. In fact, they have this concept of shame called *Hshuma.*

What is *Hshuma?*

As mentioned, *Hshuma* is the Moroccan concept of shame. Basically, Moroccans feel extreme *hshuma* once they do something inappropriate or act against the norms of their culture. With this concept of *hshuma,* if someone does something very shameful, that person may be ostracized by his/her own family or even by the entire society.

Also, the sense of self-worth possessed by Moroccans is focused externally, meaning they hold the opinions of others about them very highly. Basically, they are very conscious of how other people might perceive them.

Moroccan Family Values

In terms of family values, Moroccans hold their family very dearly. To Moroccans, their family is the most important unit of their life and they play a very important role if different social situations.

In Morocco, nepotism (hiring your own family members over other applicants) is viewed positively. According to them, this shows that you are dedicated to helping your own family.

As an individual, you must always be subordinate to your family.

Moroccans see family as both the nuclear (direct) and extended family.

All elderly people are respected and revered.

Customs and Etiquettes in Morocco

Moroccans also hold some very strict customs and etiquettes. They uphold and follow all of these in order to avoid experience *hshuma* (shame). Here is a list of some of their common customs and etiquettes that you should definitely keep in mind.

Etiquettes when you meet someone.

Moroccans greet each personally. They take the time to talk to each other, whether it is about friends, business, family, or some other topics.

Shaking hands is a customary greeting for individuals with the same sex.

Once a close relationship has already been developed and established, kissing both cheeks is allowed. Cheek kisses typically start at the left cheek while also shaking hands. This is true for women with women and for men with men.

In any greeting that occurs between a woman and man, the woman is required to extend her hand first. If she fails to do so, the man should bow his head instead in greeting.

Upon arriving at a social function, make sure to shake hands with the person on your right then continue going around the room. You should start from the right side first towards the left.

Etiquette for gift giving

When you are personally invited to a Moroccan home:

Make sure to bring nuts, sweet pastries, flowers, or figs and give it to the host/hostess.

Also, if there are any children in the home you will be visiting, you should bring a small gift for that child. This will be seen as a token of appreciation and affection.

Never bring alcoholic beverages not unless you know for sure that your host/hostess drinks them.

Etiquette when dining

When you are personally invited to a Moroccan home:

Before entering the house, make sure to take your shoes off first.

Make sure to dress appropriately and smartly. Doing this demonstrates that you respect your host/hostess.

If you have a spouse, check whether they are invited as well or not. Remember, there are some conservative Moroccans who will not entertain mixed-sex parties.

Observe proper table manners!

Again, Moroccans are also very particular about table manners. So carefully observe and keep these in mind:

The guest of honor normally sits right next to the host.

There will be a washing basin taken to the table before the meal stars. Hold out your hands right above the basin while water will be poured on them. A towel will also be provided so make sure to wash your hands using it.

Do not start eating if the host/hostess has not blessed the food yet. You also cannot start eating unless the host/hostess starts to eat.

Food is served on a communal bowl.

Make sure to take food from the bowl that is right in front of you. Do not take something from the other side. If you are a guest of honor, choice cuts will be served right to you.

Drink and eat only using your right hand.

Once the meal is over, the washing basin will be taken to the table again.

Etiquettes in doing business

Moroccans are also very particular when they do business. In fact, majority only choose to do business with someone who they respect and know. So if you want to do business with a Moroccan, make sure to spend time with them first to create a personal relationship first. Here are some Moroccan business etiquettes that you should keep in mind.

Always make an appointment first and make it in advance! Also, make sure to confirm it again a day or two before the actual meeting date.

Avoid setting meetings during Ramadan because Muslims cannot drink or eat during the day.

Never schedule meetings on a Friday particularly between 11:15 a.m. to 3 p.m. This is because most companies close their business for prayers.

French is widely used in business dealings with Moroccans however, double check to make sure since some companies use English. This will help you prepare an interpreter should you need one.

Remember, Moroccans tend to look for long-term business partners. Make sure that you are ready for that commitment.

Expect haggling – Moroccans tend to haggle a lot and they barely see any offer as final.

Moroccans tend to make decisions slowly – do not rush them! This may be seen as an insult on their part.

Men should dress themselves in business suits that dark colored and conservative.

Women should dress themselves in elegant dresses, pantsuits or business suits. They should also cover themselves suitably. Meaning, dresses and skirts should be able to cover the knees and the sleeves must cover most of their arms.

Avoid wearing any expensive or flashy jewelry and accessories.

Prepare business cards – make sure that one side is translated to either Arabic or French.

Moroccan Religion

Majority of Moroccans practice Islam as their religion. This also governs their personal, economic, political and even their legal lives. In fact in 2010, the Pew Forum estimated the religious affiliation in Morocco as 99.9% Muslim and the other 0.1% as other religious groups.

The latest estimates shows that the Marrakesh and Rabat communities have around 100 members each and that the Casablanca Jewish community is comprised of 2,500 members. Sunnis make up the majority at 67% with some non-denominational Muslims. They are the second biggest group of Muslims at about 30%.

Forms of Entertainment – Music, Sports, Architecture And Literature

Morocco is a beautiful country that is also ethnically diverse and rich in civilization and culture. In fact, since its independence, the world of entertainment in Morocco has definitely blossomed. This is true for different aspects of entertainment like literature, music, sports and even theatre. In fact, in 1956 the Moroccan National Theatre was founded and since then, it has offered regular productions of French and Moroccan dramatic works. Music and Art festivals also occur all through the during the summer months. Here are some specifics about the forms of entertainment at Morocco.

Moroccan Music

In terms of music, the origin of most Moroccan music came from Arab, Amazigh and sub-Saharan roots. Morocco is also the home of Andalusian classical music that is popular all over North Africa. There is also a genre called as Contemporary Andalusian Music which was instituted by composer/arts Tarik Banzi. He is also the founder of Al-Andalus Ensemble. As of today, popular forms of western music are also starting to become popular in

Morocco. These music includes country, fusion, metal, rock and most especially hip-hop.

Moroccan Sports

In Morocco, the most popular sport that they play is football – it is particularly popular among the urban youth. In fact, did you know that historically Morocco was the first African and Arab country to ever qualify for the FIFA World Cup second round? This was back in 1986. Also, Morocco is the home of several gold Olympic medalists such as Nawal El Moutawakel, Saïd Aouita, and Hicham El. Gold and tennis are also quite popular in Morocco and in fact, several professional Moroccan players have competed in several international competitions. Kickboxing is also highly popular in Morocco and in fact, Badr Hari, a Moroccan martial artist and heavyweight kickboxer, is one of the most famous K-1 fighters in the world.

Moroccan Architecture

As of today, a popular and new trend in Moroccan decoration is called the Moroccan style. It has roots originating from the Moorish architecture and it was made famous by the renovation in Marrakech and the vogue of the Riads. Also, due to its increasing popularity, it is now even used in some circles in the USA and in the UK! Moroccan Architecture is rich, alluring and beautiful and it is as varied as the landscape of Morocco itself. The design itself can range from elaborate with colors that are bold, to the clean, simple tones of earth colors. Other people have even described Moroccan architecture as eclectic, majestic, contemporary and exotic. The influences for Moroccan architecture come from France, Spain, Portugal and of course, from the Arab world.

Moroccan Literature

Literature in Morocco is written in French, Arabic and Berber. Some of the most influential writers like Driss El Khouri, Driss Chraïbi and Mohamed Choukri have heavily influenced many modern pets, novelists and playwrights. Other significant Moroccan authors include Leila Abouzeid, Fouad Laroui, and Abdellatif Laabi. Also, take note that orature (meaning, oral literature) is also very important for Moroccans – be it in Amazigh or Arabic.

Chapter 4: Modes Of Transportation In Morocco

If you do not own a private car that you can drive around, do not worry! There are several modes of transportation available in Morocco for you to choose from. Here is a list of transportations that you can choose from once you get to Morocco.

Petit Taxis/Grand Taxis

Majority of Moroccan cities have taxis that can drive you around the city limits. Also, there are different kinds of taxis for you to choose from.

Petit Taxis

This is a smaller car painted in a specific designated color – the color differs from one city to another. Its maximum capacity is only three people plus the driver. If you want a transfer from point-to-point within a particular city limit, a petit taxi is the best choice for you.

Grand Taxis

While petit taxis are used mainly for transportation within a specific city limit, grand taxis are used for city-to-village or city-to-city transport. Also, a grand taxi is typically shared – meaning, if you are only alone at first, the driver can choose to let other passengers ride with you. Also, a grand taxi typically does not depart unless the capacity is full – it can accommodate a maximum of four people in the rear and two people in the front seat. This shared taxi is pretty cheap but it is also uncomfortable – especially during long trips in the summer. Imagine cramming inside the taxi with six other people in a four door Mercedes without any air conditioning?

Trains

Rail transportation is also an option in Morocco. The main rail network for passenger-transport is comprised of a North to South link starting from

Tangier through Casablanca and Rabat to Marrakech. This North/South link also interconnects with the East to West connection that links Oujda in the East through Fes to Rabat. In order to check for more specific routes, make sure to find the nearest train station you can find.

Buses

Another form of transportation available in Morocco is the bus. In fact in the bigger cities like Rabat and Casablanca, they are offering public bus services. However, remember that buses can get very overcrowded, tight and hot. The routes are also sometimes hard to pinpoint. Lastly, keep in mind that tickets are normally Dh4.

Ferries

There are countless ferry crossings that operate from Spain to Morocco. Currently, these ferries are able to connect five ports in Spain to four ports located in Morocco. As a whole, there are around 39 ferry crossings every day across ten different ferry routes which are operated by seven different ferry companies. These companies are FRS, Grimaldi Lines & Inter Shipping, Grandi Navi Veloci, Trasmediterranea, Naviera Armas, and Balearia.

Bicycles

If you are just staying within city limits, and you just want to explore the direct area where you are you should also consider just renting a bicycle. There are many bicycle-renting shops at Morocco – or if you want, you can even buy one for yourself! This is perfect if you want to savor the surroundings and just sight-see leisurely. This will also help you save money on taxi or bus fares!

Chapter 5: Some Cities Of Morocco That You Can Stay At During Your Visit

Now that you are familiar with the geography, language, norms and modes of transport in Morocco, here are some cities of Morocco that you can stay at!

Rabat

This city is the administrative and political capital of Morocco and although it is not exactly a tourist spot, you should still visit it. In this beautiful city, you will be able to discover some superb colonial architecture, and boulevards lined with tall palm trees. This city is reasonably traffic free and the atmosphere exudes a cosmopolitan feel. All in all, life in Rabat is pleasant and fairly laid back.

Majority of the good accommodations in Rabat can be found in the new city between Ave. Abderrahman and Ave. Mohammed V. In the old medina you will be able to find some low-budget and affordable dives and some riads (a riad is a townhouse that is set around an inner garden). If you want to be immersed in luxury, you should definitely check out Riad Oudaya (a Bed and Breakfast place), or the 5 star Hôtel La Tour Hassan. If you are looking for something more affordable, you must definitely consider the lovely Hotel Darna.

Casablanca

Casablanca is definitely the cultural and economic capital of Morocco. It shows Morocco constantly on the move – this is the city where money is made, where art galleries flourish, and where designers can present their work. Casablanca is definitely a cosmopolitan area and is more open to Western practices. This is seen in dressing style, and in how men and women willingly hang out in beaches, bars, restaurants, and even at hip clubs.

However, you should know that Casablanca is also prone to widespread boulevards, traffic jams, and some unique community problems.

If you are looking for a place to stay at in Casablanca, do not worry! They have a lot of different inns and hotels for you to select from. You can stay at budget hotels, luxury hotels, hostels, apartments or guesthouses. It is definitely your pick. If you are looking for something affordable, you should check out Hotel Astrid but if you want to be bathed in luxury, check in at the 5 star hotel, Hyatt Regency Casablanca!

Marrakesh

Once you get at Marrakesh, you should definitely start and head right in. It is a wonderful city filled with tourist destinations you can visit. You can start at the sensational Djemaa el-Fna or you can head north towards the maze of souqs! This maze was once the area where the Berber people traded gold, leather, slaves and ivory. If you look around, you will also be able to find some new galleries and boutiques.

For a place to stay, Marrakesh also offers you a lot of choices from palaces to fleapit hotels. Just take your pick – you can either stay at budget friendly inns, ville-nouvelle hotels, or you can choose to rent an entire villa! They also have a lot of luxury resorts that you can stay at. If you are looking for something reasonably priced, check out Bab Hotel – it is 4 stars but still very cost-friendly! If you want to stay somewhere luxurious, definitely check out Ksar Char Bagh – it is a 5 star hotel and quite costly, but it is also a very breathtaking place!

These are just some of the cities of Morocco, and some hotels that you should definitely visit and stay at. However, make sure to do your own research too to ensure that you will be able to find which city you would really want to visit.

Chapter 6: Delicious Cuisine And Places To Go To In Those Cities

Now that you know of some places to stay at and some destinations you can tour and visit, you should also familiarize the local cuisine and where to find them in Morocco. Here is a short list of restaurants, cafes and etc. that you should visit for some delicious food.

Rabat

If you are staying at Rabat and currently looking for a place to eat some delicious food, you should definitely visit these places:

La Petit Beur – Tajine

They offer excellent Moroccan food from tasty couscous to luscious tajines. They also serve the best pastillas in the city!

Ty Potes

If you are looking for some French cuisine, this is the best place to go! It is a welcoming and pleasant tea house and lunch spot. They offer a wide range of savory and sweet crepês, sandwiches and salads.

La Veranda

If you are looking for something Mediterranean in taste, make sure to visit this restaurant! It is set loft-style in a modern villa surrounded by a beautiful garden and is located under tall palm trees. They also serve contemporary Mediterranean-French food bistro.

Casablanca

Casablanca is full of places and establishments that you can visit. However, here are some top restaurants that you should definitely visit:

A Ma Bretagne

If you are looking to eat some delicious seafood, this is definitely the place for you. In Africa, this restaurant is said to be the best and they definitely serve superb food! Also, although they focus on serving seafood here, you can still order some other French delicacies.

Patisserie Bennis Habous

Declared as one of the most traditional and famous patisserie in Casablanca, this place truly serves excellent food! It is the best place to visit if you are looking to eat some traditional treats of Morocco like pastillas, or some of the best gazelle horns (cornes de gazelle; almond paste).

Le Rouget de l'Isle

If you are looking for exceptional and scrumptious French food, then this is the right place for you! This restaurant is definitely one of the top eateries in Casablanca. It is sophisticated, sleek and charismatic and it is well-known for its light, simple but very delicious French cuisines. What makes this place even more amazing is that it has very reasonable prices! So make sure to visit it when you find yourself in Casablanca.

Marrakesh

If you find yourself in Marrakesh, make sure to come around these places and consume some of the most delicious foods you have ever tasted!

Villa Flore

This place is perfect if you are looking for a Mediterranean meal. In here, you will be able to eat in an art-deco, white-and-black riad with a very comforting atmosphere. They serve Moroccan salads, meltingly soft duck and lamb and some other delicious goodness.

Plats Haj Boujemaa

If you are simply looking for a café where you can rest for a while and enjoy a good light snack, then this is definitely the place for you! You can stay at a courtyard seating or simply grab a small booth and enjoy your warm bread, spicy olives or some grilled meats! They also offer some excellent yummy chips, and if you are feeling bold, you should certainly try out and savor offal.

Chapter 7: Major Events And Festivals You Should Not Miss!

If you really want to experience and revel in a full, dynamic, and exciting trip to Morocco, you should plan your trip so that you can visit it whenever there is a festival going on. Here is a list of some major events and festivals that you should definitely not miss if ever you plan to visit Morocco!

Marathon des Sables

This is also called as the Sand Marathon. It is an exhausting race that lasts for 6 days and covers about 151 miles! It is set in the Sahara desert of Morocco and 30 countries with over 600 different competitors join it every year! During the race, the competitors have to carry their equipment by themselves and they have to cook their own food. This competition usually takes place in honor of a charity. It takes place every April.

Rose Festival

If you are a fan of flowers, most especially roses, then this festival is definitely a must-see for you! It is held in a small beautiful town named Kelaa-des-Mgouna found in the Dades Valley in Morocco. This town is also the home of the largest distillery plant for rose water in Morocco! During this festival, the entire town is very colorful and fragrant, and there is a lot of singing and dancing to celebrate the successful harvest of the roses. This festival takes place in May.

Fes Festival of World Sacred Music

This is one of the major festivals celebrated at Morocco. It is a very spiritual festival that is held yearly in Fes. During this festival, you will be able to bump into different mystics, dancers, and chanters from all over the world! You might even bump into some spiraling dervishes coming from Iran! The Fes festival will definitely be a very unique experience for you. It combines popular entertainment, high art, intellectual challenges and a high spiritual energy. This festival takes place in June.

Essaouira Gnawa Music Festival

This is another major festival celebrated at Morocco. Basically, it is a music festival that is based on the traditional music of Gnawa. However as of today, during the festival itself, several musicians and artists from all around the world are also featured. This is a very successful yearly festival and it has been around for a decade now! Also, the venue changes from year to year and it is scattered all around the beautiful town of Essaouira. During this festival, you will be able to enjoy a combination of Gnawa music, acrobatic dancing and you might even see some religious rites! This festival takes place in June.

Popular Arts Festival in Marrakech

Again, this is another major festival celebrated in Morocco. This Popular Arts Festival in Marrakech is in fact able to attract performs of all kinds. From professional dancers, to folk singers, some hailed fortune-tellers, fire-swallowers, clever acting troupes, snake charmers and more! All of these performers come from different parts of Morocco and they show of their talents during this festival. However, since the year 2000, the Popular Arts Festival has also fascinated a lot of entertainers and artists from Asia and Europe.

Because of this, this festival is now open to performers who live outside of Morocco! Normally, the main events and attractions occur in the 16th Century ruins of the Djemma el Fna (the central town square) and the ruins of Badi Palace. Also during this festival, one thing that you should not miss is the *Fantasia* that takes place in the exterior city walls during nightfall. *Fantasia* is a horse-riding display that shows hundreds of different charging horsemen and women who are wearing the traditional horse-riding clothing. This festival takes place in July.

Eid ul-Adha after Ramadan

Lastly, this is one of the most important festivals celebrated all throughout Morocco. Basically, Eid ul-Adha translates to Festival of Sacrifice. During this festival, Muslims commemorate Ibrahim (Abraham) and the trial he had to go through where Allah asked him to sacrifice his only son. To honor the show of faith that Ibrahim displayed during that time, Muslims slaughter an animal – typically a goat or sheep. The meat gathered during this slaughter is mostly handed away to other people. Eid ul-Adha occurs seventy days once Ramadan ends and after the Hajj (Mecca pilgrimage) is completed. This festival takes place in October.

These are just some of the major events and festivals that take place in Morocco. Although some of these festivals are sacred to the Moroccan people and honors their religion, you can still take part in it as long as you remain sincere. Also, if you are a big fan of flowers, music, dancing and art, the annual music and art festivals that takes place in Morocco is something that you really should not miss. So if you truly want to experience Morocco to the fullest, make sure to plan your trip around these festival months!

See you in Morocco!

We hope you have enjoyed and learned some fascinating facts from this travel guide. Keep everything in this tour guide in mind and have an awesome, memorable and unique stay in the Kingdom of Morocco! Have a safe and happy journey!

Experience Everything Travel Guide Collection™

EXPERIENCE EVERYTHING
PUBLISHING

www.ingramcontent.com/pod-product-compliance
Lightning Source LLC
Chambersburg PA
CBHW060044040426
42331CB00032B/2279